POWERING UP A CAREER IN
ARTIFICIAL INTELLIGENCE

MAX WINTER

ROSEN
PUBLISHING®
New York

Published in 2016 by The Rosen Publishing Group, Inc.
29 East 21st Street, New York, NY 10010

First Edition

Library of Congress Cataloging-in-Publication Data

Winter, Max.
Powering up a career in artificial intelligence/Max Winter.
    pages cm.—(Preparing for tomorrow's careers)
Includes bibliographical references and index.
ISBN 978-1-4994-6089-6 (library bound)
1. Artificial intelligence—Industrial applications—Vocational guidance—
Juvenile literature. I. Title.
TA347.A78W56 2016
006.3023—dc23

2014044690

Manufactured in the United States of America

CONTENTS

Introduction 4

CHAPTER ONE
NEW FRONTIERS IN ARTIFICIAL INTELLIGENCE 8

CHAPTER TWO
EDUCATION FOR A CAREER IN ARTIFICIAL INTELLIGENCE 16

CHAPTER THREE
A CAREER IN ROBOTICS 24

CHAPTER FOUR
A CAREER IN VIDEO GAMES 32

CHAPTER FIVE
A CAREER IN SEARCH ENGINES 39

CHAPTER SIX
GETTING YOUR START IN ARTIFICIAL INTELLIGENCE 48

CHAPTER SEVEN
THE FUTURE OF ARTIFICIAL INTELLIGENCE 58

Glossary 68
For More Information 70
For Further Reading 73
Bibliography 75
Index 78

INTRODUCTION

A group of researchers in Bangladesh have developed software that can detect how users of a computer are feeling. How does the program do this? It analyzes how fast they are typing and also looks at the words they use. A hotel in California is currently doing tests for a robot that, given the right commands, can take packages from the front desk to guests' rooms. At Harvard, software is being developed that helps professors out by grading their papers for them. All of these developments are examples of the ever-growing presence of artificial intelligence (AI). Can machines think like humans? Artificial intelligence experts think so. Since the invention of the very first computer, the goal has been to make machines that can think.

As early as the thirteenth century, people have been trying to create thinking machines. Majorcan philosopher Ramon Llull employed logic and complex

The room-sized ENIAC was an early computer used by the U.S. Army. Technicians are programming it in this 1946 picture.

mechanical techniques in an attempt to convert Muslims to Christianity. In the seventeenth century, the philosopher and mathematician Gottfried Leibniz argued that all reasoning could be reduced to an ordered combination of elements. It is the theoretical ancestor to modern artificial intelligence.

However, one of the first examples of artificial intelligence in action proved to be a hoax. In the eighteenth century, a machine called the Turk was believed to be able to play chess as well or better than any human. It was a machine in a box with a chessboard on top. The upper half was a mechanical mustachioed gentleman wearing a turban. For years, the Turk beat most of its opponents, but it was later discovered that the box with the machine also housed a real-live chess player who controlled the mechanical man on top.

About 150 years later, the Electronic Numerical Integrator and Computer, or ENIAC, the first successful problem-solving machine, was put into use by the U.S. Army. The machine was huge. It consisted of forty panels, each 2 feet (61 centimeters) wide, 2 feet (61 cm) deep, and 8 feet (2.4 meters) high. There were also 18,000 vacuum tubes, 70,000 resistors, 10,000 capacitors, 6,000 switches, and 1,500 relays. The machine took up an entire basement at the Moore School at the University of Pennsylvania. Its size made it impossible to use anywhere else. Regardless of its physical awkwardness, many were dazzled by it. ENIAC was the first machine to be able to perform calculations that humans used to do by hand.

Fortunately, developments in computer science also meant smaller and more manageable machines.

International Business Machines Corporation, or IBM, was the first company to develop a widely used, functioning computer. In the 1960s, IBM was making 70 percent of the world's computers with the main function of processing numerical data. As technology changed, smaller computer companies joined the field and added new features like workstations, networks, and a graphic interface. Soon, Apple and IBM became the leading computer manufacturers, each trying to best the other by providing more and more functions to make life easier and more organized. At the back of computer designers' minds was a perpetual question: What more can this machine do? How can I modify it to make it more appealing to consumers? Can this machine think?

Will we ever reach a point where we can automate many of the tasks that take up our day and have them taken care of by a machine? Smartphones certainly make life easier for many people, with reminders and applications that make it possible to, for instance, deposit a check in a bank account. But this sort of function is still slightly short of the goal of artificial intelligence: to create a machine that is as complex, as multifunctional, and as capable as the human mind at its best. With each new development, scientists inch closer and closer to this goal. And as they do, the field of artificial intelligence becomes more tempting to an increasing number of people.

INTELLIGENCE

The smartphone is the latest foray into artificial intelligence that satisfies the average consumer's need. The first smartphone was designed by IBM and sold in 1993. It had a touch screen interface, calendar, address book, calculator, and a few other functions. As computer memory improved and integrated circuits became less expensive, smartphone capabilities also increased. Now Internet access, data storage, and features such as augmented reality—in which a smartphone's global positioning system (GPS) can be used to overlay a phone's camera view with information about the surrounding area—are almost standard features.

Many smartphones also feature digital assistants

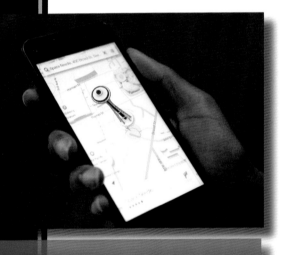

The map on Amazon's Fire Phone uses 3D renderings of buildings.

that use voice recognition to process a request and then respond to it. This is one example of the ways that artificial intelligence devices are finding their way into daily life. It works like this: the user asks a question, and then the program either makes a calculation, finds the information requested using a search engine, or performs a function to satisfy the speaker's request. There are currently three types of smartphone digital assistants on the market. Siri is made by Apple; Microsoft's assistant is called Cortana; Google's assistant is Google Now. All three companies put a lot of programming power into creating assistants that not only answer requests, but also do it with flair. Microsoft, for example, used screenwriters to script some of Cortana's responses to make the assistant both funny and informative.

THE HISTORY OF DIGITAL ASSISTANTS

Digital assistants have a history long before the smartphone. One of the first was Microsoft Bob, an animated dog search assistant that was created for use with Windows 3.1 in 1995. The assistant was poorly received by customers and eventually became Clippy, an animated paper clip office assistant that popped up in Microsoft applications, such as Word or PowerPoint, to ask if the user needed any help. Users could then type in a question for the assistant to answer.

Another incarnation of personal assistants were PDAs (personal digital assistants), which were devices specifically designed to hold calendar appointments, contacts, notes, and reminders. All had keyboards, and some came equipped with pens that could take notes on-screen. These were popular from 1980 to about 2000.

FROM GAMES TO THE WORKPLACE

Scientists and programmers are constantly developing ways in which artificial brains can make our lives easier. One example is the cognitive technology supercomputer Watson. Watson was designed by IBM to be a contestant on the game show *Jeopardy!* in 2011. It won against champions Brad Rutter and Ken Jennings with four terabytes of stored data. Currently, Watson is used as and is considered a piece of cognitive technology. The user asks Watson a question, and Watson provides an answer based on its best analysis of data from numerous search engines. The interesting thing about Watson is that its abilities increase with time. It actually learns from both correct and incorrect responses, gradually developing the ability to answer different and more complex queries successfully. AI scientists are realizing, gradually, that they can use this technology to complete certain actions that used to require specialized knowledge—such as doing legal research—far more efficiently, faster, and cheaper than before. A program called Kodak Alaris, to give another example, could change the way insurance claims are processed. This software would store pictures

IBM's Watson computer competes against Ken Jennings and Brad Rutter on *Jeopardy!*

of different kinds of documents in its memory and then use those images to sort and process different kinds of insurance claims at many times the speed of a human being. As such projects become more and more commonplace, artificial intelligence may change the face of the modern workplace.

ARTIFICIAL INTELLIGENCE AND HEALTH CARE

Health care robots are being used in hospitals to care for patients. One robot called Paro looks like a baby seal and is being used to interact with hospital patients. This robot, the eighth generation of a design from a Japanese company, uses five different sensors to perceive the people and environment around it. The robot recognizes light and dark, can feel touch, and identifies where a voice is coming from. It also learns through its interactions with people. So if a person does not like something Paro does, it will learn not to do that again with that particular person.

AI IN EDUCATION

Artificial intelligence also seems like a natural partner for education. Some schools are using a computer-based grading system that actually reads handwritten essays. However, some feel that the computers do not have the same human touch that a person does and that it's possible for kids to learn how to beat the computers with essays that use certain key words.

At the Massachusetts Institute of Technology, scientists have been developing another essay-grading machine called the Enhanced AI Scoring Engine, or EASE. Unlike previous computer-based grading systems, this machine works by using the actual scores given to real professors' graded essays as models for its own scoring. Once enough professors' criteria have been entered into the software, EASE "learns" how to grade essays. The program isn't foolproof, and it has plenty of critics—including Seth Perelman, who generates fake essays with his own AI-driven software and feeds them into EASE to show that the program will give nonsense text a high score—but with development, it could make education quite different by taking teachers' focus away from grading tests and placing it more on classroom instruction.

SELF-DRIVING CARS

Artificial intelligence machines are even driving cars, as evidenced by the self-driving car, currently being perfected by Google. This revolutionary technology operates by analyzing potential situations one might encounter in traffic and instructing the mechanism inside the automobile—the steering wheel, the engine, or the ignition—to respond accordingly. It winds its way through different traffic situations with acute sensors in its front and its back, which notice objects in the vicinity, calculate accordingly, and send commands to the car's "brain." The car, which spent decades in development, is currently in its testing phase; it

Although there is a person driving this Google self-driving car, the car has been tested on streets without a driver.

has been taken on experimental drives on city streets and has proven to be successful in driving itself. The potential benefits of such a vehicle would be huge. With automated cars, accidents caused by driver error or impairment would be eliminated. There are also benefits to the disabled. They would be able to travel from place to place independently, entirely without assistance. Self-driving cars would also potentially free up the time of drivers, allowing them to concentrate on other tasks.

The field of artificial intelligence is changing every day, mainly driven by public demand. A career in this field requires the right training and educational background. There are clearly many different facets to this field. If you have an interest in a career in AI, you have a wide range of choices. Are you interested in creating AI machines that enhance people's lifestyles? Do you want to work on educational programs? Maybe your interest is in making a machine that mimics a human being in every way. These are the exciting choices available to you in the artificial intelligence field.

CHAPTER TWO

EDUCATION FOR A CAREER IN ARTIFICIAL INTELLIGENCE

Training for a career path in artificial intelligence begins as early as high school. A very firm grounding in mathematics and computer programming is essential. This would lay the groundwork for understanding college-level courses in these areas.

ESSENTIAL CLASSES

At the most basic level, you will need to master algebra, geometry, trigonometry, and calculus. These skills will provide significant grounding for you as you move forward in your studies.

Additionally, you will need to study computer science. Most computer science classes will teach you something about the history of computers, as well as focus on instruction in basic programming. Computer science is required in many high schools at an introductory level. Students who are particularly interested in the field can take elective courses to continue their studies. Colleges with a strong computer science department look for applicants who have taken as many basic courses as possible.

A solid foundation in both mathematics and science in high school will help you as you apply to colleges for a computer science degree.

EXTRACURRICULAR ACTIVITIES

What you do with your time outside of the classroom is also important for honing your skills and showing college admissions departments your level of interest. Find out if your high school has any clubs or societies that involve your area of interest. Perhaps there's a robotics club or computer science club. Or maybe just a science club—you could find a way to make that useful for your future career, as well. Even a math club would be helpful. Competing in math contests is another way to sharpen your skills and show that you would be a good candidate for a college-level computer science program. You can even take courses in computer science at a local community college. Any extra effort expended in this direction would only improve your college application.

Don't forget to use your summer break wisely! In the last twenty-five years, numerous summer camp programs have cropped up that allow students interested in computer science, math, and, yes, even artificial intelligence to study what they are passionate about and meet other kids who share that passion. Space Camp, which has been hosting kids to study space travel during the summer since 1982, recently launched Robotics Camp, at which young scientists study the building of robots and familiarize themselves with the workings of artificial intelligence. A number of kids who have attended this camp, based at the U.S. Space and Rocket Center, have gone on to work for NASA.

SCIENCE FAIRS

Science fairs are an excellent way to showcase your talent in the field of AI. Many of these fairs, especially if they're held at the state level, attract people who work in the sciences. If you were noticed by an AI professional at a young age, it could not only help you get into the college of your choice, but it might also

The Intel International Science and Engineering Fair is held each May. The grand prize is a $50,000 college scholarship.

give you a leg up in your career! There are several science fairs that operate at a national level.

The USA Science and Engineering Festival takes place each year in Washington, D.C., with numerous exhibits, panels, and speeches spanning several days. Visitors might see exhibits at this fair ranging from flight simulation to the special equipment used by the Central Intelligence Agency (CIA).

ROCK THE SCIENCE FAIR

The toughest part of being in a science fair is figuring out what project you'd like to enter. If you're interested in artificial intelligence, there are all kinds of projects you might try. For instance, one basic principle of artificial intelligence involves having a machine choose a response from a set of possible responses. To assemble a set of these responses, you could take a survey in your class of your fellow students' favorite songs. Then, you could program a playlist for the class based on their top survey responses, as well as suggestions that they would enjoy. Or you could do what two competitors in the 2012 Google Science Fair did and create a virtual competitor for simple math-based computer games. The competitor's name was Bob. The two entrants found that when Bob was playing a game, the human players tried harder and performed better. These sorts of results are what encourage further study of, and progress in, artificial intelligence.

Each year, seven million students compete to attend the Intel International Science and Engineering Fair. Only around 1,800 are chosen. The attendees come from over seventy countries to hear speeches and presentations on topics ranging from physics to artificial intelligence.

The Google Science Fair began in 2011 and is sponsored by Google, Lego, Virgin Atlantic, National Geographic, and *Scientific American*. The competition is free and open to students from around the world age thirteen to eighteen. It covers eleven categories, from computer science and earth science to food science and studies of flora and fauna.

MAKING CONNECTIONS

You can also connect with other people who share your interest in AI online. Email lists, or LISTSERVs, are public forums on which people with a common interest can discuss any subject. When you sign up for a LISTSERV, you get every e-mail that is sent to the group. Members may send questions as well as updates or new information relating to the LISTSERV main topic. Alternately, you could join or create a makerspace. Simply put, a makerspace is a place where people make things together; by sharing ideas, resources, knowledge, and experience, everyone benefits. They tend to be focused on creating with technology. Makerspaces may be anywhere, really. You will often find them at public libraries or recreation centers, but they may also be found online.

Engineers inspect a robot that was created to do investigative and recovery work in a nuclear power plant.

Internships are another option for connecting with AI professionals. There may be some opportunities open to you in high school, but many more opportunities will open up to you as a college student.

An internship is an opportunity for you to work in a company and learn on the job. It can be a fantastic way for you to find out how different kinds of artificial intelligence companies operate. While the tasks you might perform as an intern might be very simple, that doesn't matter; any chance you have to see artificial intelligence experts in action should be taken. The best place to start looking for possible internships is in your library; your librarian should be able to guide you to the right resource. If there are companies you are specifically interested in, check their websites to see if they offer internships and what the application process is. Remember that some internship opportunities are very competitive. Just because you apply for an internship does not mean you will get one.

CHAPTER THREE

A CAREER IN ROBOTICS

Robotics is the field most likely to make use of artificial intelligence. Although scientists and computer programmers have made a lot of progress since the beginnings of this field, we still have a long way to go before realizing the dream of creating a robot with artificial intelligence. The earliest types of robots—some of which are still in use today—don't look like C3PO from *Star Wars*, by a long shot; they look like blocky machines, with long arms, controlled by humans. However, as robotics becomes more advanced, the machines become more advanced as well. For example, roboticist David Hanson, in recent years, has designed a robot that looks, speaks, and, some say, acts like science fiction writer Philip K. Dick.

HIGH SCHOOL AND COLLEGE COURSES FOR BUDDING ROBOTICISTS

Because of the advanced nature of robotics, in order to become a full-fledged roboticist—a scientist who designs, builds, and experiments with robots—with an eye toward including artificial intelligence in the construction, you would need a PhD. The path toward

Chris Borer, a student at Carnegie Mellon University, has spent years developing snakelike robots that can search for people in collapsed buildings.

getting such a degree would start with an undergraduate degree in computer science. If you have a specific career path in mind—say, robotics, video game design, or working at a search engine, which we'll discuss later— it's a good idea to tailor what you study to suit this goal.

In high school, you would want to take as many math courses as possible, such as algebra, geometry, calculus, and trigonometry, as these subjects are the basis for any computer science degree. It's best to try to take advanced classes since you will take these courses at the college level as well. Taking advanced classes in high school may make you exempt from some of them at the college level, freeing your time to take other courses related to your desired profession. You would also want to take computer science courses to familiarize yourself with programming language.

In college, you can prepare for an advanced degree in robotics with a more basic degree in computer science, which is offered at many schools, with specializations in both robotics and artificial intelligence. For the typical computer science major, most courses toward the degree are required, though, a certain number would be electives. A person interested in robotics—and, specifically, robotics related to artificial intelligence—would need to take elective courses that pertained specifically to these interests. This would benefit both your own personal education and your résumé; in a sense, these courses would serve as job training. A computer science bachelor's degree from an accredited university would include required coursework such as computation, programming, algorithms, data structures, and basic systems courses. Students typically have a wide variety of choices for electives, which would allow you to choose the courses that will best prepare you to build and program robots. These courses may include classes in computing, basic artificial intelligence (perhaps slanted toward problem solving), and cyberphysical systems—mechanisms that combine computer software with machine parts.

Alternately, some schools, such as the Carnegie Mellon Robotics Institute, might let you minor in robotics for your bachelor of science (BS) degree. A minor is an area of specialization that is different from your major. A minor in a particular field would mean taking a certain number of classes in this area of study, though it would be fewer classes than a student would take for his or her major. Beyond basic introductory courses, a student could take a number of electives, such as classes in perception and cognition, combined with any more specialized artificial intelligence courses.

ADVANCED ROBOTICS STUDY

A minor in your undergraduate studies provides a good foundation, but from there, you may want to pursue a master of science degree (MS) and, possibly, a doctoral degree (PhD). Both master's and PhD students need to be able to work independently, in addition to excelling in coursework. Much of a master's and PhD program involves individual research. Coursework would continue in areas such as perception, cognition, automation, mechanical engineering, and mathematics—along with a selection of electives. The research and independent work of a master's candidate would build toward a final presentation or dissertation, which would determine whether or not a student will be awarded his or her

Student Irvin Cardenas controls the movements of TeleBot, a version of a RoboCop that is being tested at Florida International University.

degree. It's a lot of pressure! PhD programs consist of more independent research and less coursework. A typical master's program takes two years, while a PhD program can take up to five or six years. PhD candidates can present their final dissertations and research studies to potential employers.

WORKING IN ROBOTICS

The kinds of artificial intelligence jobs you can get in robotics vary depending on your degree. With a bachelor's degree, you could get a job as an engineer. Engineers are responsible for a wide range of duties, such as fine-tuning brand-new robotics projects that still have minor bugs in their operations. They might help to construct equipment for entertainment use—as in a museum or at an amusement park. They might also come up with new ideas

A ROBOTIC HAND WITH ITS OWN SENSE OF TOUCH

After ten years of work, the **NEBIAS** project is finally complete. NEBIAS is a prosthetic hand with a very delicate sense of touch. This project's goal was to design a prosthetic hand that could function as accurately as and with the sensitivity of a real hand. Scientists employed technology that closely resembles artificial intelligence. Sensors in its surface pick up information about physical objects that they touch: their shape, their texture, and whether they're soft objects or hard objects. The sensors send this information to the brain. The brain sends a signal to the nervous system, and then the user controls the hand's movements. The hand could revolutionize current prosthetic limbs as it has far more functionality and even feeling.

Kapil D. Katyal, an engineer at Johns Hopkins, demonstrates a robotic hand that has been developed for wounded soldiers. The project is from DARPA, Defense Advanced Research Projects Agency.

for robotic innovations. Right now, some robots are being developed to study the effects of global warming. Others are being fine-tuned to make the work done in factories, such as those that manufacture airplanes or automobiles, which requires the transport of heavy equipment, more smooth and efficient.

With master's degrees, engineers have more responsibilities and more influence over planning, creating prototypes, and final design. Some job titles that someone with a master's degree might be qualified for include robotics engineer, controls engineer, and robotic programmer. Many people with PhDs in robotics work in labs on theoretical work after getting their degrees, which means that they may work on concept robots, many of which are not for everyday use. People with PhDs also tend to go into teaching at the university level. As a professor of robotics, you would be responsible both for teaching undergraduate and graduate students and for guiding research projects—as well as generating projects of your own for further study.

Some robotics projects allow researchers to let their imaginations run wild, while others have more serious, practical applications, such as robots built for use in the medical arena or the military. However, all projects require a great deal of knowledge and dedication. Daniel Lee, who received a PhD from the Massachusetts Institute of Technology, has worked on quite a few outlandish projects in his career, among them a self-playing xylophone and a robotic dog that turned toward you when you called its name.

CHAPTER FOUR

A CAREER IN VIDEO GAMES

People who design video games are commonly called video game designers or programmers. Companies that produce them are typically called video game studios. Increasingly, as games become more complex, video game studios are making use of artificial intelligence to make their games more challenging and more fun. A whole subset of video games has developed in the last twenty-five years called role-playing games. These games take players into scenarios much like those they might see in the movies. The decisions the players make affect the course of the game— and that is where artificial intelligence comes in. Programmers "teach" games to react in a certain way, depending on players' behavior.

A BACHELOR OF SCIENCE IN COMPUTER SCIENCE

Game designers or programmers need to have a solid computer science background. They typically major in computer science in college with a focus on game design and artificial intelligence. Some colleges have courses in both game design and artificial intelligence, and some do not, so be

Gamescom is the largest fair for computer games.

sure to check a college's course offerings as you research where you would like to go to school. A BS in computer science comes with a list of required courses, such as calculus and algebra. Computational ability is required for programming at any level and would be particularly important if you were working with games that involve probability. A bachelor's degree would also require a grounding in statistics and what academicians call the theory of probability, which is a branch of science that attempts to explain the laws behind statistics themselves. Note that some colleges require students to take courses in other sciences, so you may have to take classes in biology, physics, and chemistry as well.

For the gaming part of your major, basic courses in programming, computing, and software development would be needed to point you in the right direction for the rest of your studies. Additionally, you would need to take courses that would teach you about different kinds of operating systems, such as those associated with PCs and those associated with Apple computers. You would also study what is called Internetworking, or the nuts and bolts of the ways computers "talk" to each other over the Internet. You would take courses in computer graphics, game design, and artificial intelligence. Some colleges offer the option to study digital art and animation so that students can learn how to draw the two-dimensional images commonly used for these products.

ADVANCED DEGREES

More advanced jobs in the field require an advanced degree with more intense coursework. If you choose to continue past a BS, you could either pursue a master of science degree (MS) or a doctorate (PhD). You would probably have to take a course in algorithms, which are the equations that decide, ultimately, how video games and online games behave; you would also need to take a course in 3D graphics. As

Laurie Haack from Raytheon speaks to students and leads them in brainstorming activities at California State University, Fullerton's Women in Engineering Program.

games have developed, some designers have moved toward a more realistic appearance for the people, creatures, and background scenes. Beyond the basic requirements, you would then have a choice of which courses you might take to further tailor your education to suit your interests. Some colleges offer other elective courses in artificial intelligence and game design. It may even be possible to take a class that allows you to develop your own game! For the more specialized part of the MS, you would want to focus on courses related to cognition. Cognition is the study of mental abilities, including the processes related to knowledge, memory, judgment, and evaluation, among others. These courses would teach you how to create characters for different kinds of games, particularly those in which players assume roles. Courses like these would also give you the tools to make the characters you create "think" using artificial intelligence.

For a PhD in computer science, with a focus on artificial intelligence in gaming, you would need to spend four years, at the minimum, primarily devoted to a research project in your field. You would have minimal coursework, but the courses would cover a broad range of computer science topics. As a PhD student, your success or failure depends entirely on your level of dedication to your studies and your project, as well as your persistence. You should, of course, choose a project that would make a significant contribution to your résumé.

WORK EXPERIENCE

A great deal of artificial intelligence work is done by programmers. There are different ranks of programmers, each with their own set of responsibilities. A junior programmer, for instance, may help fine-tune a game already in existence or work out problems that come up, such as those reported by end users during beta testing. Issues the junior programmer might deal with include graphic

COMPUTERS THAT DESIGN GAMES BY THEMSELVES

Angelina, a new program designed by British researcher Michael Cook, actually designs its own games given a set of characteristics to work with. If the program is fed a one-word idea, it does the rest, creating characters, a landscape, and rules all by itself. It does this, in part, through Internet research. If you give it the key word "danger," for example, it would look that key word up in a search engine and assign images and other characteristics to the game based on the most common associations with that word.

SANTA'S SNOWFIGHT ESCAPE!

Press Space To Begin

Santa's Snowfight Escape! is one of the games created by the artificial intelligence Angelina.

quirks (such as the appearance of the characters or scenery in a game) or bugs in the system that cause a game to malfunction. A lead programmer would be one level above a junior programmer. The lead programmer would usually be in charge of a team of juniors, guiding their work and educating them as needed. The lead programmer would have to be an expert in coding as well as be able to make decisions that affect a project, including determining what projects a company should devote time and money to developing. Programming positions also exist for the graphic parts of games, for their audio effects, and for the "tools" component—the nuts and bolts that make the games run efficiently. For a job specifically addressing artificial intelligence issues, an MS would be required. One such position might be that of the artificial intelligence programmer. This position would combine knowledge of several things: basic programming techniques and probability to evaluate the possible directions players in a game might take and the most efficient way to solve a problem, from both an economical and visual standpoint.

CHAPTER FIVE

A CAREER IN SEARCH ENGINES

D oing a web search is an activity that is as basic to most computer users today as turning on the machine in the first place. Searching for information online seems to be quite simple: You type in a search term, wait a few seconds, and then look through the results the search engine offers you. Some will be useful, and some will not be useful. The search engine will normally arrange these results in order from most useful to least useful. Although getting a result from a search engine is a near-instant process, the work that goes on behind the scenes is anything but instant. It involves the careful, dedicated work of hundreds of engineers, programmers, and other personnel. And certain parts of a search engine's workings have a great deal to do with artificial intelligence. For instance, many of the "decisions" a search engine makes about which entries to offer you first involve information synthesis that is above and beyond normal levels of calculation. Additionally, the larger search engines, such as Google, are immersed in research projects all the time that make use of the most recent artificial intelligence discoveries.

THE RIGHT EDUCATION FOR THE JOB

Training for a job with a search engine such as Google starts with a basic education in computer science. Take as many computer science courses as possible in high school, and make the best use of your spare time to pursue your interests through clubs, special projects, contests, and even extra classes, if possible. College training for a career as a search engine employee with a focus on artificial intelligence is slightly different from the other AI career paths. There are a few basic areas in which you would have to have advanced knowledge. An undergraduate degree in computer science would, of course, include classes in calculus and physics. If possible, you should try to take a computation course as well as a cognition course. Cognition courses are offered by the psychology department, and coursework focuses on the study of how people think, learn, and remember information. As part of this degree, courses in programming and electronics are required. A course in optimization, which has to do with how individual members of a set might be chosen, according to a set of criteria, is a good elective if your college offers it. Other basic courses would include programming, algorithms, computation, and systems, but you would want to pay special attention to the courses that focus on systems (design and engineering) and algorithms. A course in systems covers how search engines are constructed, including the hardware and tools used to build a computer. A course in algorithms would help

A career in search engine artificial intelligence includes understanding how people think and interact with various devices, which would help produce the best end-user experience.

you understand how search results are chosen and presented after a search. You might, at a certain point, be required to put yourself on a particular track, or course of study. You would either want to put yourself on the artificial intelligence track or the systems track. If possible—and some colleges let you do this—you might want to combine the two to give yourself the best possible preparation for working at a search engine.

BEYOND A BACHELOR OF SCIENCE

If you wanted to secure a more advanced job at a search engine, you would probably think that an advanced degree is the best way to get it. But not so fast! This is where the issue of educational background gets a bit complicated. One of the most senior employees—and the person in charge of hiring—at Google, Laszlo Bock, has said, in a 2014 *New York Times* article "How to Get a Job at Google," that the five most important qualities for a Google employee are learning ability, leadership, humility, ownership, and expertise. Learning ability, in this case, means being capable of noting your mistakes and figuring out how not to make them more than once, as well as absorbing new information quickly. Being able to lead others well while also having a realistic sense of your own strengths and weaknesses is also key. When Bock uses the word "ownership," he means being able to take responsibility for the outcome of your own projects at work. Expertise, for Bock, is simply the degree of experience and knowledge you bring to the work you do. At Google, managers are interested in workers who have an acute, irreplaceable familiarity with a subject. When you think about it, these are qualities that would help you in any job—not just a position at a search engine.

You might note that Bock does not mention education as part of his five most important qualities. In the same article, he reports that 14 percent of some teams at Google are made up of people with no college degree at all, and that number is rising.

Laszlo Bock (*left*) is pictured with another Google employee, Jason Grishkoff, at their human resources offices in Mountain View, California.

But, of course, a degree, especially an advanced one, is helpful. A bachelor's degree is often the minimum qualification for many software engineering positions—however, the hiring personnel for these jobs prefer applicants with a master's degree, or MS. MS candidates can choose a couple of different areas to specialize in, such as systems and artificial intelligence. Courses in both of these areas will cover a broad range of topics, such as computation, human-computer interaction, and software theory. Because the very definition of a search engine suggests considerable breadth of knowledge and information gathering, you would want to make sure that your own education was as well-rounded as possible.

A SOFTWARE ENGINEER

What do people who work at search engines do, exactly? As someone with an interest in artificial

Jobs in artificial intelligence often involve working as part of a team.

intelligence, you would most likely work as a software engineer on a small team. The job of a software engineer involves using ideas from every

WHAT'S GOING ON AT GOOGLE X?

If you've spent much time learning about Google, you'll notice that its list of special projects is always growing and always changing. Increasingly, the common thread running through many of its projects is artificial intelligence. Google is particularly interested in using artificial intelligence to empower robots. Much of the research it does toward this goal is completed in a lab called Google X. Not much is known about how Google X works—because Google itself has kept its activities highly guarded. The facility is headed by Sergey Brin, one of Google's founders, and a man named Astro Teller. Astro Teller's official title, in all honesty, is captain of moonshots. Moonshots, at Google, are projects that many would call highly improbable—but these projects could change society irrevocably if they are successful. Sound like a fun job? It is—but it's also highly challenging. The core of the activities in the lab, as with all artificial intelligence research, is to make a machine think just like a human does—and when you're working with a mechanism that has as much information in reach as Google, the possibility of reaching this goal seems ever closer.

facet of computer science. Engineers look at how information is retrieved, artificial intelligence, how machines can learn and process language, system design, networking, and security. They also work on designing a highly functional and simple user interface, among many other things. Because engineers often work together, the ability to cooperate—and also to compromise—is very important. But the ability to stay focused on a goal is also very important.

CHAPTER SIX

GETTING YOUR START IN ARTIFICIAL INTELLIGENCE

There are many different types of jobs in artificial intelligence. As you prepare to do a job search, the most important thing is to keep your final goal in mind. What is it you want to do with artificial intelligence? Do you want to work as a roboticist? Do you want to design video games? Do you want to help search engines function more smoothly and efficiently? And how high do you want to rise in your industry or in a company? All the research you do about employment in this field should start with those questions—and the information you gather should, optimistically, provide answers for them.

BEFORE THE JOB SEARCH

One of the first things you need to do before you start looking for an actual job is write a résumé. Your résumé can and should change depending on the jobs you apply for. You might showcase more of one strength or skill that suits one job, and less of another skill that has nothing to do with the job you are applying for. But what is a résumé? A résumé is a concise description of your skills and education. For most people, it should just be one page. Usually, at the top, you give your background: where you went to school, where you live, what awards you won. Then, beneath that, you state your work experience. When you're young, many of the things you might put on a résumé might not be jobs. They might be internships, descriptions of research projects you worked on with a professor, or offices you held in high school or college organizations. The most important thing about a résumé is the way you present yourself. The résumé must tell hiring personnel, almost from the first glance, why they should hire you. And to do that, the résumé needs to be well organized. Group information such as your educational experience, your club affiliations, and your internships under separate headings. Your résumé should also put your accomplishments in plain view. If you have something you would like to brag about, don't be shy! Add it to your list of credits. If you had a position, of any type, that involved a responsibility you are proud of, include it. If you have a special skill, such as technological expertise, include this information as well. Make sure that the reader of your résumé knows what you can do and can sense how well you can do it by the pride you show in yourself with your résumé.

INTERNSHIPS AND THE JOB HUNT

Once you begin looking for a job, things become more complex. There are many ways to find jobs, and no one method is better than another, so long as you get results. As a high school and college student, you might have the best luck with applications for internships. An internship, though it may not pay anything, is an excellent way to find out about the field you're looking to enter and make connections with people working in that field who may help you in the future. There are plenty of places to find out about these positions. A guidance counselor or faculty advisor can usually point you to internships in your chosen field of study. You can also try your school library's reference section. There may be compiled information about both local and national internship possibilities. You can also search online. Just remember to be as specific as possible. Use key words like "artificial intelligence," "computer science," and "internship." You should also add your location

Students like these Google interns have to get through a complicated application process, but they get an opportunity to learn hands-on from major companies.

to make the search more useful. Another way of looking for an internship is simply to check the website of a company you're particularly interested in. If a company offers such positions, it usually offers specific instructions about applications.

Once you've settled on a place to apply to, you'll need to write a cover letter. This letter is your chance to introduce yourself to a possible employer. It expresses your purpose for contacting that employer— to look for an internship. And it's also a place where you can summarize your skills. If you felt that your leadership skills, combined with your organizational abilities, were your strongest points, you could mention that in the cover letter. If you have an accomplishment that you're proud of, make sure you mention it. This sort of detail, mentioned in a cover letter, could be the thing that causes an employer to pull your résumé out for a second look.

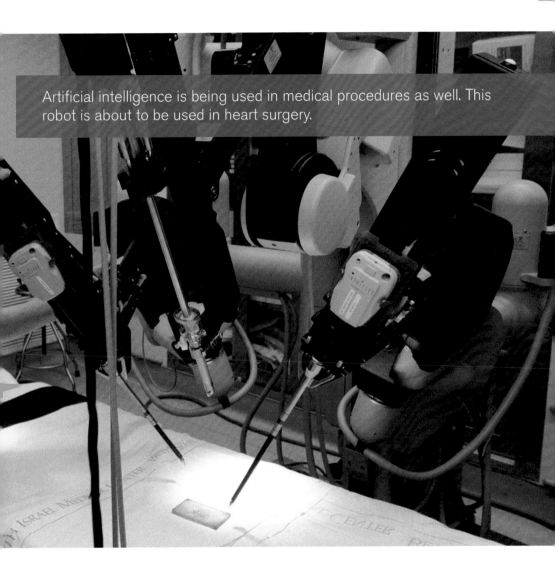

Artificial intelligence is being used in medical procedures as well. This robot is about to be used in heart surgery.

Internships are generally fairly simple jobs, and if they do pay, they often don't pay very much. The great value of an internship is that it helps you learn more about the industry you want to work in and it helps you make connections within that industry. Additionally, and perhaps most importantly, it is the first step toward

FINDING A MENTOR

At any job or internship, you're going to have a supervisor. Different supervisors have different styles. Some are very conversational and like to give their employees lots of feedback about their performance, while others are more distant. You will find, the more you work, that you will feel more kinship with some supervisors than with others. If there is one supervisor that you like in particular, you should try to learn as much as possible from that person. This sort of relationship is called a mentorship. A mentor is a kind of teacher who can show you how a job is done, introduce you to other people in his or her field, and, most important, help you make connections that will help you in the future. There is an old saying "It's not what you know, it's who you know." Most employers want to hire people who are recommended by people they either know personally or respect. And so having a mentor is a first step toward making yourself an appealing potential employee.

an entry level job. For this reason, you should try to perform well and learn as much as you can. Making a good impression on your supervisors can pay off when you start looking for a real job.

Whether you're applying for an internship or a full-time job, you will have to go through an interview. This is a chance for you to get to know a possible employer and for the employer to get to know you. More importantly, it's the employer's opportunity to determine whether you are right for a job or internship at the company. There are some things you can do to help an interview go well. You can dress professionally. That means no jeans, sneakers, or T-shirts. However, in most cases, you don't have to go as far as wearing a suit. Many companies have employee profiles, and you can see how other people at the job dress to indicate what you should wear to an interview with that company. During the interview, it's important to show confidence by making consistent eye contact, expressing yourself clearly, and engaging with your interviewer. Ask questions about the job. Show that you are interested—not only in what you can do at the job but also how you can learn from it. The most important thing you can do during an interview, in the long run, is this: appreciate yourself, your strengths, and your abilities. If you go into the conversation with a clear head and with pride in your accomplishments and your worth, chances are good the employer will be able to tell.

When you are applying for jobs and when you are actually employed, it's important to think about the long term. Remember that you may need to start

The HRP-2 robot is controlled by human brain activity using a brain machine interface (BMI). The robot is designed to learn the user's movements in order to help disabled or elderly people.

small to get the high-ranking job you seek. A person who wanted to become a video game designer at a big firm, for instance, might start out at a smaller studio and work his or her way up. Constantly be conscious of your performance. A good performance at a job, regardless of how small the job might be, could get you a positive recommendation that may lead to your next position. And the more positive recommendations you have, the more likely it is that you will eventually land the job you want.

CHAPTER SEVEN

THE FUTURE OF ARTIFICIAL INTELLIGENCE

As time has passed, and work on artificial intelligence has continued, the goals scientists have in mind become increasingly imaginative. Beyond simply making life more efficient through artificial intelligence, its developers are now trying to complicate its uses, spreading them through every part of our lives. Can you imagine robots that compose music? What about merging microchips with human DNA? How about machines with human personalities and emotions? And what about fighter planes that are controlled, in part, with computer "brains"? Some scientists can, and they are moving toward making these ideas into realities. The way there is complicated, and not everyone is in favor of these developments, but as they proceed, it will be fascinating to watch the world slowly change.

SONG-WRITING ROBOTS

If you were to tell anyone, even as recently as twenty-five years ago, that someday robots might

Beethoven and Johann Nepomuk Maelzel were said to have enjoyed using musical automatons in the 1800s. However, this 1815 metronome was a more common musician's tool and is still used today.

write songs, they might not believe you. But today, some French and American scientists, working for the giant music company Sony, are making this particular feat a reality. Certain musical artists have a very distinct style that can be detected by even a casual listener. Having a computer detect and imitate an artist's style begins, like so many technological accomplishments, with elbow grease and analysis. The work begins when the scientists break down music—by classical composer Johann Sebastian Bach, jazz great Charlie Parker, or even by pop music icon Paul McCartney of the Beatles—into its most basic components: notes. The scientists look at everything, mapping it all out: the way notes form chords, the way chords build melodies, and then finally the way the finished composition sounds. The engineers then feed this information into a computer. The computer does its own form of analysis, coming up with algorithms that can improvise melodies. The software will imitate the characteristics it sees in the music, creating songs and compositions that are much like something the original artist might have composed, based on all the patterns observed. Scientists hope that soon, the computer will be able to judge whether its melody is close to being like one from the original composer. The ideas behind this technology are centuries old. Musician and inventor Johann Nepomuk Maelzel created musical automatons that were powered by bellows back in the 1800s. Ludwig van Beethoven, who was a fan of this technology, actually used the automatons between symphonies and concerts in 1813!

A ROBOT THAT CLEANS THE HOUSE

Everyone has, at one time or another, wanted some help cleaning the house. What if a robot could help you? Researchers at Stanford have, for the past several years, been working on a robot called Stanford Artificial Intelligence Robot, or STAIR, that could do just that. The robot could wash dishes, clean rooms, clear tables, and do other household chores with maximum efficiency. It would be of primary use for the elderly and disabled at first, though it might be expanded to use by the general public in the future. Though the idea sounds fairly futuristic, it is entirely within today's scientists' grasp.

ARTIFICIAL LIFE

Movies, from *2001: A Space Odyssey* to *A.I. Artificial Intelligence* to *I, Robot* and more, have suggested to us that someday there will be robots that think, act, and look so much like humans that we may not be able to tell the difference. A group of scientists is on the way to fulfilling that promise with a project

Will Smith starred in the science fiction thriller *I, Robot* in 2004, a movie based on the premise that a robot acting alone has committed a crime.

called Cosmic Beings. These Beings will be made through the merging of human DNA with nanotechnology, which it operates at a scale much smaller than a microscopic scale. The scientists are trying to mimic the intricacies of human cell structure with human-made materials. The actions each cell takes to keep itself functional would be imitated as well, the idea being that anything the human body can do, a machine can do better because it is invulnerable. One of the goals of this project is to use these Cosmic Beings to colonize other planets. In order for this to happen, space exploration would have to be far enough along that the proper experiments could be undertaken to see if such a development were possible. Some scientists have suggested that the development of artificial intelligence in this direction could transcend what we know as evolution, as humans build better and better bodies that we can inhabit ourselves. Above and beyond these factors lies this reality: the Cosmic Beings would be immortal, and scientists would have successfully discovered a way to guarantee eternal life. However, there is debate about whether the Cosmic Beings can be said to be alive at all. Regardless of the outcome of the debate, this is an exciting step, not only for artificial intelligence but also for life on this planet.

ARTIFICIAL INTELLIGENCE IN THE MILITARY

While in some areas, artificial intelligence is being combined with human beings to create new kinds of life, in other areas, artificial intelligence is being used to eliminate the need for human beings in dangerous and high-stress situations. In the

An Unmanned Combat Air System (UCAS) is being demonstrated over the flight deck of the aircraft carrier USS *George H.W. Bush*.

future, it may even shape the way we fly. Pilot error, especially during military combat, can mean the difference between life and death. Currently, both the Navy and the Air Force are working on artificial intelligence copilots that allow pilots to concentrate on fewer tasks, which could potentially give them an advantage during missions. The F-X fighter, currently in development, could eventually replace the Air Force's best plane. The Navy has created the X-47B drone, which can land itself on an aircraft carrier. The Navy has demonstrated how this drone can fly right alongside human pilots with a test flight during which both humans and drones flew separate planes in formation. The hope is that by 2030, robot copilots could fly alongside remote-controlled pilots, keeping all military personnel safe on the ground.

THE FUTURE FOR ARTIFICIAL BRAINS

World-famous physicist Stephen Hawking, though he acknowledges the obvious benefits of developing machines that can think, feel, and behave with the depth and complexity that humans possess, also feels that our development of technology could eventually mean replacing DNA-based life. Unlike the scientists who believe in nanotechnology to fix humans, Hawking has said that intelligent machines will be the things that reach out to the stars and colonize other planets (as the Cosmic Beings are meant to do). Some computer scientists, such as Canadian Hector Levesque, consider artificial intelligence far too fallible; they do not consider any machine, regardless of its complexity, anything more than a machine. Though they are capable of complex calculations and data accumulation, simple common sense eludes them. Simple anaphoras, which use two expressions, one of which helps explain the other, are impossible for current machines to comprehend. For example, a machine could not readily identify the "it" in the following sentence: "Alyssa threw the clay at the wall, and it broke apart easily." Most people would recognize that the "it" refers to the clay, not the wall, since clay is something that breaks apart easily. Computers, however, would not.

Critics such as Hubert Dreyfus think computer scientists are not using the correct definition of "brain" or "mind" when they think about artificial intelligence—and that the term "artificial intelligence" itself is a contradiction. Whatever critiques it may spark, artificial intelligence is a fascinating field of study and endeavor, the ramifications of which will remain unpredictable for many years to come.

GLOSSARY

algorithm A series of steps with which a problem is solved.

artificial intelligence Computer technology that can imitate human thought.

cognition The way in which computers acquire and store information.

computation The solving of problems by a programmed machine.

Cosmic Being A computer in which human DNA has been fused with microchips by means of nanotechnology.

graphics The images that computer programs and software present to the user.

Internetworking The practice of connecting computers to each other through networked systems.

internship A position at a company, usually unpaid, in which a person learns the basic parts of a job.

LISTSERV A community sustained by e-mail communication on a specific topic.

makerspace A location, either virtual or physical, in which individuals can gather to work on projects.

mentor A person who teaches or advises another person about a craft or profession.

microchip A tiny semiconductor that carries a significant amount of circuitry.

nanotechnology The creation and engineering of circuits and other mechanisms at a microscopic level.

programming Creating commands that tell a computer how to behave.

résumé A document that supplies information about a job applicant's background and experience.

robotics The study, construction, and development of robots.

search engine Software, powered by the Internet, that retrieves information for users based on key word terms.

studio A company that designs small technological projects, such as video games.

systems In computer science, either the connected mechanisms within a computer that make it run or linked computers that "talk" to each other to transmit information.

virtual Existing only within the domain of a computer.

FOR MORE INFORMATION

Association for the Advancement of Artificial
Intelligence (AAAI)
2275 East Bayshore Road
Suite 160
Palo Alto, CA 94303
(650) 328-3123
Website: https://www.aaai.org
The AAAI is a nonprofit scientific society that was
founded in 1979. It seeks to advance scientific
understanding of intelligent behavior in machines
with research and responsible use of artificial
intelligence.

Canadian Artificial Intelligence Association (CAIAC)
Department of Computer Science
University of Regina
3737 Wascana Parkway
Regina, SK S4S 0A2
Canada
(306) 585-4700
Website: https://www.caiac.ca
The CAIAC is dedicated to the promotion of interest in
artificial intelligence. It conducts workshops as well
as an annual national conference, and it sponsors
the journal *Computational Intelligence*.

Georgia Tech Institute for Robotics and Intelligent
Machines (IRIM)
801 Atlantic Drive

Atlanta, GA 30332-0280
(404) 385-8746
Website: http://robotics.gatech.edu
IRIM is a research institute built on the work of the
    Robotics & Intelligent Machines Center. The institute
    launched in 2013 and aims to bring together robotics
    researchers throughout Georgia Tech University.

Institute of Robotics and Intelligent Systems (IRIS)
CLA H 1.1
Tannenstrasse 3
8092 Zurich
Switzerland
Website: http://www.iris.ethz.ch
The Institute of Robotics and Intelligent Systems (IRIS)
    is part of ETH Zurich, a university in Switzerland.
    It is made up of seven research laboratories where
    various aspects of robotics, such as nanodevices for
    biomedicine, are studied.

MIT Computer Science and Artificial Intelligence
    Laboratory (CSAIL)
The Stata Center, Building 32
32 Vassar Street
Cambridge, MA 02139
(617) 253-5851
Website: http://www.csail.mit.edu
CSAIL is the largest research laboratory at MIT, and
    its members are focused on developing innovative
    information technology. Its members have launched
    more than one hundred tech companies.

Robotics Industries Association (RIA)
900 Victors Way
Suite 140
Ann Arbor, MI 48108
(734) 994-6088
Website: http://www.robotics.org
Robotics Online, the RIA's website, provides
    information to help engineers, managers, and
    executives use robots and automatons. The site
    presents industry insights, technical papers, and
    more.

WEBSITES

Because of the changing nature of Internet links, Rosen Publishing has developed an online list of websites related to the subject of this book. This site is updated regularly. Please use this link to access this list:

http://www.rosenlinks.com/PTC/Artif

FOR FURTHER READING

Barrat, James. *Our Final Invention: Artificial Intelligence and the End of the Human Era*. New York, NY: St. Martin's, 2013.

Blackford, Russell, and Damien Broderick. *Intelligence Unbound: The Future of Uploaded and Machine Minds*. Hoboken, NJ: Wiley, 2014.

Bostrom, Nick. *Superintelligence: Paths, Dangers, Strategies*. New York, NY: Oxford University Press, 2014.

Brynjolfsson, Erik, and Andrew McAfee. *The Second Machine Age: Work, Progress, and Prosperity in a Time of Brilliant Technologies*. New York, NY: Norton, 2014.

Ceceri, Kathy. *Making Simple Robots: Exploring Cutting-Edge Robotics with Everyday Stuff*. Sebastopol, CA: Maker Media, 2014.

Flach, Peter. *Machine Learning: The Art and Science of Algorithms that Make Sense of Data*. New York, NY: Cambridge University Press, 2012.

Foreman, John W. *Data Smart: Using Data Science to Transform Information into Insight*. Hoboken, NJ: Wiley, 2013.

Hamm, Kelly III, John E. Hamm, and Steve Hamm. *Smart Machines: IBM's Watson and the Era of Cognitive Computing*. New York, NY: Columbia University Press, 2013.

Harbour, Jonathan S. *Video Game Programming for Kids*. Independence, KY: Cengage, 2012.

Kurzweil, Ray. *How to Create a Mind: The Secret of Human Thought Revealed.* New York, NY: Viking, 2012.

McEwen, Adrian, and Hakim Cassimally. *Designing the Internet of Things.* Hoboken, NJ: Wiley, 2013.

Rose, David. *Enchanted Objects: Design, Human Desire, and the Internet of Things.* New York, NY: Simon and Schuster, 2014.

Russell, Stuart, and Peter Norvig. *Artificial Intelligence: A Modern Approach.* New York, NY: Pearson, 2010.

Shalev-Shwartz, Shai, and Shai Ben-David. *Understanding Machine Learning: From Theory to Algorithms.* New York, NY: Cambridge University Press, 2014.

BIBLIOGRAPHY

Bagley, Caitlin A. "What is a Makerspace? Creativity in the Library." ALA TechSource, December 20, 2012. Retrieved November 12, 2014 (http://www.alatechsource.org).

Chang, Angela. "The Robot Butler Cometh." *PC Magazine*, January 10, 2007. Retrieved November 12, 2014 (http://www.pcmag.com).

CNN Money. "15. Video Game Designer." November 12, 2013. Retrieved November 12, 2014 (http://money.cnn.com).

Friedman, Thomas L. "How to Get a Job at Google." *New York Times*, February 22, 2014. Retrieved November 12, 2014 (http://www.nytimes.com).

Gertner, Jon. "The Truth About Google X: An Exclusive Look Behind The Secretive Lab's Closed Doors." *Fast Company*, May 2014. Retrieved November 12, 2014 (http://www.fastcompany.com).

Guizzo, Erico. "How Google's Self-Driving Car Works." IEEE Spectrum, October 18, 2011. Retrieved November 12, 2014 (http://spectrum.ieee.org).

Hochberg, Dan. "When Robots Write Songs." *The Atlantic*, August 7, 2014. Retrieved November 12, 2014 (http://www.theatlantic.com).

Hornyak, Tim. "Lost Philip K. Dick android back with loud shirts." CNet, January 15, 2011. Retrieved November 12, 2014 (http://www.cnet.com).

IBM. "The birth of the IBM PC." Retrieved November 12, 2014 (http://www-03.ibm.com/ibm/history/exhibits/pc25/pc25_birth.html).

IBM. "What is Watson?" Retrieved November 12, 2014 (http://www.ibm.com/smarterplanet/us/en/ibmwatson/what-is-watson.html).

Kodak, Inc. "How to Accelerate Insurance Claims Processing By Up To 90%." June 25, 2014. Retrieved November 12, 2014 (http://graphics.kodak.com).

Kolowich, Steve. "Writing Instructor, Skeptical of Automated Grading, Pits Machine vs. Machine." *The Chronicle of Higher Education*, April 28, 2014. Retrieved November 12, 2014 (http://chronicle.com).

Marcus, Gary. "Why Can't My Computer Understand Me?" *The New Yorker*, August 14, 2013. Retrieved November 12, 2014 (http://www.newyorker.com).

Markoff, John. "'Beep,' Says the Bellhop. Aloft Hotel to Begin Testing 'Botlr,' a Robotic Bellhop." *New York Times*, August 11, 2014. Retrieved November 12, 2014 (http://www.nytimes.com).

Markoff, John. "Essay-Grading Software Offers Professors a Break." *New York Times*, April 5, 2013. Retrieved November 12, 2014 (http://www.nytimes.com).

McMullan, Thomas. "Ghosts in the Machine: How AI Research is Bringing Game Characters to Life." *The Guardian*, October 14, 2014. Retrieved November 12, 2014 (http://www.theguardian.com).

Nusca, Andrew. "How Apple's Siri really works." ZDNet, November 3, 2011. Retrieved November 12, 2014 (http://www.zdnet.com/blog/btl/how-apples-siri-really-works/62461).

Penn Engineering. "ENIAC: Celebrating Penn Engineering History." Retrieved November 12,

2014 (http://www.seas.upenn.edu/about-seas/eniac).

Prisco, Giulio. "Cosmic Beings: Transhumanist Deism in Ted Chu's Cosmic View." IEET, February 12, 2014. Retrieved November 12, 2014 (http://ieet.org/index.php/IEET/more/prisco20140212).

Schofield, Jack. "The Keyboard of the Future Will Know Just How You Feel." ZDNet, August 31, 2014. Retrieved November 12, 2014 (http://www.zdnet.com).

INDEX

A

algorithms, 26, 34, 40, 60
Angelina, 37
Apple, 7, 9, 34
artificial intelligence, applications of
  education, 12–13
  health care, 12
  housework, 61
  military, 64, 66
  music, 58, 60

B

bachelor's degrees, 26, 27, 29,
  32–34, 42
Beethoven, Ludwig van, 60
Bock, Laszlo, 42
Brin, Sergey, 46

C

Central Intelligence Agency, 19
cognition, 27, 36, 40
computer science, 21, 25, 26,
  32–34, 36, 40, 47, 50
Cook, Michael, 37
Cosmic Beings, 63–64
coursework, 16, 24–27, 32–34,
  40–41
cover letters, 52

D

digital assistants, 8–9

E

Electronic Numerical
  Integrator and
  Computer (ENIAC), 6
engineers, 39, 44–45, 47
Enhanced AI Scoring Engine
  (EASE), 13
extracurricular activities, 17–18

G

global positioning system (GPS), 8
Google, 9, 13, 20, 21, 39, 40,
  42, 46
Google Science Fair, 20, 21
Google X, 46
graphics, 7, 34, 35, 38

H

Hanson, David, 24
Hawking, Stephen, 66

I

Intel International Science and
  Engineering Fair, 21
International Business Machines
  Corporation (IBM),
  7, 8, 10
internships, 22–23, 49–50,
  52–55
interviews, 55

78

K

Kodak Alaris, 10–11

L

Lee, Daniel, 31
Leibniz, Gottfried, 6
Levesque, Hector, 66
LISTSERVs, 21
Llull, Ramon, 4

M

Maelzel, Johann Nepomuk, 60
makerspaces, 21
master's degrees, 27, 29, 31, 34, 44

N

NASA, 18
NEBIAS project, 30

P

Paro, 12
Perelman, Seth, 13
PhDs, 24, 27, 29, 31, 34, 36
programmers, 10, 24, 31, 32, 36, 38, 39

R

résumés, 26, 36, 48–49, 52

robotics, 18, 24–31, 48
Robotics Camp, 18
Rutter, Brad, 10

S

science fairs, 18–21
search engines, 9, 10, 25, 48
  careers in, 39–47
self-driving cars, 13–15
software engineers, 44–45, 47
Stanford Artificial Intelligence Robot (STAIR), 61
systems, 26–27, 34, 40–41, 44

T

Teller, Astro, 46

U

USA Science and Engineering Festival, 19

V

video games, 25, 48, 57
  careers in, 32–38

W

Watson, 10

ABOUT THE AUTHOR

Max Winter is a writer who lives in New York City.

PHOTO CREDITS

Cover Jens Schlueter/Getty Images; cover (background), back cover, p. 1 Lukas Rs/Shutterstock.com; p. 5 Time & Life Pictures/Getty Images; pp. 8, 25, 28–29, 30, 33, 50–51 © AP Images; p. 11 Ben Hider/Getty Images; pp. 14, 19 Bloomberg/Getty Images; p. 17 fstop123/ E+/Getty Images; pp. 22, 56–57 Yoshikazu Tsuno/ AFP/Getty Images; p. 35 © Michael Goulding/The Orange County Register/ZUMA Press; p. 37 Courtesy Michael Cook; p. 41 Volodymyr Grinko/iStock/ Thinkstock; p. 43 Peter DaSilva/The New York Times/ Redux; pp. 44–45 PeopleImages.com/Digital Vision/ Getty Images; pp. 52–53 Chris Hondros/Newsmakers/ Hulton Archive/Getty Images; p. 59 Musee de la Musique, Cite de la Musique, Paris, France/Bridgeman Images; pp. 62–63 © 20th Century Fox/Entertainment Pictures/ZUMA Press; pp. 64–65 U.S. Navy photo by MC2 Timothy Walter; cover and interior pages design elements Zffoto/Shutterstock.com, Sergey Nivens/ Shutterstock.com, elen_studio/Shutterstock.com, Lukas Rs/Shutterstock.com, Nucleartist/Shutterstock.com, Georg Preissl/Shutterstock.com, Jack1e/Shutterstock .com, Sfio Cracho/Shutterstock.com.

Designer: Michael Moy; Editor: Tracey Baptiste; Photo Researcher: Karen Huang

5